# How To Calm Down

## EVEN IF You're Absolutely, Totally Nuts

### 20TH ANNIVERSARY EDITION
### REVISED & UPDATED

*Do people tell you to relax and calm
down but never tell you how?
Here's how—in clear, everyday language.
And plenty more.*

"This simple yet practical book shows you how to calm down, become clear and then perform at your best. It's truly amazing!"

—BRIAN TRACY, WORLD'S FOREMOST SALES TRAINER & AUTHOR OF FOCAL POINT

"Fred's work is like having the ancient wisdom of Deepak Chopra summed up a la Garrison Keillor's Prairie Home Companion."

—ROBERT G. ALLEN –CO-AUTHOR OF THE ONE MINUTE MILLIONAIRE AND NY TIMES BEST SELLING AUTHOR.

"Your excellent presentation gives doctors life balancing methods to use with their patients and, gratefully with themselves."

—DR. CHARLES BLUM–PRESIDENT OF SOTO-USA, CHIROPRACTIC ASSOCIATION

"I wish I'd had How to Calm Down…to give to all the people I've counseled in the last two years who have been affected by layoff stress. Not only is it easy to read; it gives simple instructions that stick with you."

—CHRISTINE DORMAIER-PRESIDENT, EDUCATION BROKERS NORTHWEST,INC.

"How to Calm Down…is accessible and valuable to many, many people."

—CAROLYN LOPER-PROGRAM DIRECTOR OF THE WELLNESS COMMUNITY

"Fred is a wonderful teacher. You will greatly benefit from his ideas!"

—ROGER VON OECH, AUTHOR OF A WHACK
ON THE SIDE OF THE HEAD

"The art of relaxation is but one of the many levels to which Fred Miller speaks in this book. You will experience each of them as you follow his path to greater serenity and peace of mind."

—MORRIS NETHERTON-AUTHOR OF
THE NETHERTON METHOD

"I can meditate! I can quiet my mind and feel myself relax. I can take a time-out to just be. I tried to learn these skills several times by reading, as well as by personal instruction, but it was Fred Miller's book that worked the magic."

—SELMA PATENT-AUTHOR, LECTURER, HOMEMAKER

"The wisdom of the east in user friendly English. A powerful guide to stress reduction"

—LARRY PAYNE, PHD, CO-AUTHOR OF YOGA FOR
DUMMIES AND YOGA RX. DIRECTOR, INTERNATIONAL
ASSOCIATION OF YOGA THERAPISTS

# How To Calm Down

## EVEN IF You're Absolutely, Totally Nuts

### 20TH ANNIVERSARY EDITION

### REVISED & UPDATED

## FRED L. MILLER

Forward by Mark Bryan
author of the Artist's Way at Work

NAMASTE PRESS
a division of Namaste Information Services

*How To Calm Down Even If You're Absolutely, Totally Nuts?*
(20th Anniversary Revised & Updated Edition)

Copyright © 1999, 2004, 2008, 2009, 2000, 2022 by Fred L. Miller

Cover Design © 2022 by Fred L. Miller
Formatting, Cover Art and Design by TeaBerryCreative.com

Published by Namaste Press, a division of Namaste Information
Services, Los Angeles, CA

Edited by Ellen Kleiner, Marcia Jacobs and Barbara DeWitt Smith

Back cover photo: Jeff Davis

Library of Congress Cataloging: 98-67094
ISBN Print: 978-0-9665275-1-3
ISBN Digital: 978-0-9665275-2-0

First Printing

Have questions or want more information regarding
HOW TO CALM DOWN
EVEN IF YOU'RE ABSOLUTELY, TOTALLY NUTS?
http://www.howtocalmdown.com

*This book is dedicated to everyone
who checks their watch
two minutes after checking their watch,
who flies through two dozen TV channels
during one commercial break,
or whose mother always said to them,
"Slow down! You're gobbling your food."*

# Acknowledgments

Thank you to those who have helped me from the beginning, as well as along the way: Mildred and Lyle Miller, Kim Mandernach Miller Struthers, Sidney Galanty, John Cholakis, John W. James, Marshall Karp, Gary Kraftsow, Ellen Kleiner, Sharon Trocki-Miller, Marcia Jacobs, Sean Casey Leclaire and Barbara DeWitt Smith.

# Contents

## Part 3: Going Deeper

# Foreword

I first met Fred Miller twenty-five years ago when my longtime mentor and dear friend, Julia Cameron, introduced him to me as a friend of hers. We spoke briefly, and I remember being particularly impressed by two things: one, that he was a yoga teacher, which surprised me because he looked more like a banker than an Indian mystic, and two that he possessed a refreshing candor, saying what needed to be said in the immediate moment instead of reciting or expecting rote answers. It was Fred's character that first led me to him as a friend, and then as a teacher.

The power of *How to Calm Down* lies in its simplicity, as well as in Fred's uncanny ability to bring us to a new place before we realize we have left the old one. Because of this, I keep it on my desk for those days when a nasty blowup is lurking just beneath my emotional horizon, when I am living in the past or the future instead of the eternal moment, or when I need to flip my gratitude switch from a glass half empty to one half full.

I also find it comforting that Fred's techniques are thousands of years old and part of every major spiritual tradition, not just a modern psychological quick fix. As a result, they can be used and reused and somehow always remain fresh. It is the practicality and universality of the techniques that first attracted me to this book, and the kindness underlying each message that keeps me coming back for more. Compassion, as they say, is the highest value - and indeed, this book will introduce you to your more compassionate self.

As a teacher myself, I am acutely aware of other teachers. In fact, it was while watching Fred teach that I discovered endearing aspects of his character. He has the humor and compassion to guide students past their fears, and the confidence and strength to "stand in the fire" of students' doubts without relying on dogma to get them through the rough spots– all this while gently inviting them to become more fully who they really are.

Fred's combination of strength, grace, and commitment to "walk his talk" are why I asked him to join my teaching team years ago. Now, whenever possible, he takes part in the regular curriculum of The Artist's Way at Work seminars that I teach around the world. *How to Calm Down...* is much like Fred's teaching: it meets you where you are and guides you easily through the experience of change.

Before you know you have been taught anything, you are responding to the world differently from when you started, even if you were "absolutely, totally nuts" when you began.

Now take a deep breath, and enjoy.

Mark Bryan

# How To Calm Down

### EVEN IF You're Absolutely, Totally Nuts

## 20TH ANNIVERSARY EDITION
## REVISED & UPDATED

### The Path to Peace of Mind

# FRED L. MILLER

### PART ONE

# Starting Out

# 1

## Here & Now

Do you really want to relax?

Don't you work better when you have a full head of steam? I used to think so, but that is no longer true. I've learned that sometimes a full head of steam gets in my way.

You can achieve this by focusing on the moment, the Here & Now. The Buddhists call it mindfulness. Or being in the present moment or simply paying attention.

The job itself does not matter—you could be frosting a cake or hanging a picture—as long as you're focused, but if your mind wanders, you might smash your thumb.

You can think of this relaxation stuff as preventive medicine, or you can think of it as being race-tuned, operating at your highest level.

My name is Fred, and I was nuts. I used to be Absolutely Totally Nuts 24/7, but now not very often. I've been teaching How To Calm Down for more than thirty-five years. I teach cancer-support groups, in senior centers, third-year medical students, and attorneys. I've seen minor miracles, from a lawyer in a $2000 suit who couldn't stop jiggling his leg, to a woman undergoing chemotherapy, with real concern about her future health, settle into the Here & Now. They learned how to live one breath at a time and have a peaceful life. You don't have to become a Buddhist or a yogi or a hermit to learn to relax and enjoy your life. I learned, they learned, and so can you. It's easy: you just have to do it. One breath at a time.

At any given moment during a typical day, does your blood pressure rise, your pulse rate hit 10% over normal, and your breathing seem to stop? Sound familiar? If so, read on.

Once upon a time, I worked in a New York City advertising agency. Some days between the workload, the personalities, and the office politics, by midday I was absolutely, totally nuts. To relax at lunch, I went to a Midtown restaurant for a couple of beers and a cheeseburger. The beer solution worked. I calmed down. I was ready to face the second half of my day. After two months, however, I had put on weight. My pants were too tight and I felt terrible. I knew I had to cut out the two bottles of beer but I didn't know how to calm down without them. I then began asking other people how to relax. They told me to go to Las Vegas. Go fishing. Get a date. None of these ideas would have helped me during my lunch hour.

Other people's solutions were good for them, but not for me. I started noticing what I did when I was trying to calm down. Having abandoned the two-beer plan, I smoked a cigarette, which seemed to help, though initially I could not figure out why. Smoking, it turned out, was an abbreviated version of my first beer at the restaurant. First I stopped what I was doing at the time—that is, I took a break. Next my attention shifted from the jumble of thoughts racing through my mind to the one simple action of lighting a cigarette and taking a deep breath. Ahhh, relaxation.

All I was looking for when I began my quest for relaxation was peace of mind. I was frazzled. I wasn't running my life; instead, it was running me. I was the proverbial hamster scooting along as fast as I could on the Wheel of Life and never getting anywhere. I needed a break.

What I found was much more than that. When I began to practice relaxation, my life began to change. I slowly stopped needing outside things and became more productive. Sometimes in my life I have been fearful of new people or unfamiliar situations. Now I have developed more faith and confidence in myself, so much so that my outlook on life turned from negative to positive. Although I remain convinced that fear is part of the human condition, by regularly practicing relaxation, I found a way not to be stopped by fear but rather to move through it. Best of all, in learning to quiet my mind, I came upon a calmness deep within me. Reaching into that calmness, I could hear the voice of my true self, which is in tune with all things in the world—maybe even in the universe. In other words, I discovered that relaxation brings about a sense of well-being and contentment.

Finding an enjoyable approach to relaxation was not easy, however, especially since I had never stuck long with anything I didn't like. I had to sift through a lot of styles that didn't work before finding one that did. After reading dozens of books and attending twice as many seminars on relaxation and stress management, I borrowed some methods and invented others. Then I synthesized the most effective ones into a series of short exercises, which you will find in the pages of this book.

If your partner, child, best friend, or doctor has been harping at you to calm down and relax, or if you yourself have been feeling the need for more serenity, then you will undoubtedly find some of these exercises helpful. They may even inspire you to want to relax. Best of all, you can practice them anywhere, even while sitting back in your easy chair.

You've even heard the announcement from the airline flight attendant, "If the oxygen masks deploy, if you are traveling with a child, put on your mask first, then assist the child."

Get it? You can't help others before you have taken care of yourself. In our case, it means setting up a simple routine that keeps us mentally race-tuned for peak performance.

## YOUR PEAK PERFORMANCE REQUIRES CLEAR, FOCUSED THINKING.

*Now, here is the Secret!*

Would you like to feel better in less than ten seconds? If so, try the following exercise, called "Three Slow Breaths." As you do, keep your eyes open, and don't stop reading.

Inhale.
Now exhale.
Feels good, doesn't it?

Don't stop reading.
On your next breath, take a deeper inhale.
Hold it and count to one.
Make this exhale a little longer than you usually do.
Stop at the end of this exhale and count one.

Next, inhale even a little more deeply than last time.
Hold the inhale for two counts.
Very slow exhale this time.
Hold after exhale for two counts.
Now return to normal breathing.

### *What just happened?*

You stopped worrying for ten seconds! Your concentration was on your breath, which keeps you in the present moment. For those ten seconds you were Here & Now. You were not reliving a fearful experience from the past nor were you projecting into a future in which that fear would repeat. With your attention on your breath, you were experiencing the power of the present moment. For ten seconds you were not worried about losing your job, a sick relative, your child's report card or the day you will die. You were in the present moment. Here & Now.

Welcome to peace of mind and to presence of mind. Welcome to a state of fearlessness.

If you're anything like me, you scan the table of contents looking for the chapter that tells you how it's done, the secrets, the answers and the keys to the kingdom. Why? Because you want answers now!

So there's your answer. Now you know how to calm down and how to use three slow breaths to bring peace of mind. Good news–this breath exercise will work for you anywhere, at any time.

Try doing it ten times in the next twenty-four hours—at work, on the phone, in the so-called express lane at the supermarket, in traffic, in an elevator, at a restaurant when your three-minute egg hasn't arrived after ten minutes. And don't worry; no one will know what you're doing.

Interestingly, the human mind is capable of more than 60,000 thoughts a day, and given free rein, more than 90% of them are the same ones we had the day before. Repeatedly reliving the past can keep us stuck in old worries, fears, and frustrations. Paying attention to what's around us, on the other hand, will snap us back to what's happening right now.

*Do you know how much you think even when you think you're not thinking?*

To get a sense of the useless thoughts that fill our heads, try "Not Thinking" (Exercise I). The results are sure to be memorable.

---

## EXERCISE I

# Not Thinking

This exercise will show you how thinking can distract you from relaxing. Read it through first, then give it a try.

Sit comfortably, whatever that means for you. Kick back on the couch with your feet on a hassock or pull the lever on your recliner.

Take three slow breaths.

» Inhale. Now exhale. Don't stop reading.
» On your next breath, take a deeper inhale. Hold it and count to one. Make this exhale a little longer than you usually do. Stop at the end of this exhale and count one.
» Next inhale just a little more deeply than last time. Hold the inhale for two counts. Very slow exhale this time. Hold after exhale for two counts. Now return to normal breathing.

Breathing slowly and easily, close your eyes
for thirty seconds and Don't Think.

---

How did it go...not so hot? Was your mind racing for twenty-nine and a half seconds? If so, congratulations—you're human! We all have minds that want to race a mile a minute, hurtling out of the here and now and into the there and then. Thinking is the enemy of relaxation.

When I first started practicing this exercise, my mind was full of chatter: my voice, my ex-wife's, my boss's, the last song I'd heard on the radio. I was having conversations, even arguments, with people who weren't in the room with me! Not wanting to hear those voices yakking at me anymore, I decided to find something to do to quiet my mind. The simple techniques described in the next several chapters did the trick.

It will get better; the yakking will slow down... that's a promise.

# 2

# Getting Started

Stress and tension clog up our minds with useless thoughts. Who has stress and tension? Nearly everyone. Why? Because most of us don't know how to release the steam that accumulates inside us, day after day.

Have you ever caught yourself thinking that you are the only safe driver on the highway, that everyone else is crazy and trying to kill you by cutting you off and then slamming on their brakes? A near-accident will make us tense, sending a jolt of adrenaline through our nervous system. When we are scared of becoming another roadside fatality, even if the fear lasts only a second, our body senses danger. Our heart starts to race, our blood pressure skyrockets, and we prepare for action.

This fight-or-flight response once served a useful purpose. A prehistoric caveman, upon suddenly meeting up with a saber-toothed tiger, needed lots of adrenaline to make his next move. Heart thumping, veins bulging, he would either tangle with the creature or run for his life, and in the process release the "steam" that got him going.

People in danger today, however, can neither fight nor flee. When we're stuck in traffic, we cannot get out of the car and slug the driver who cut us off and we certainly can't run away. Actually, there is no physical outlet for our extra adrenaline, no release valve for our rapidly pumping hearts.

Here's another example of how we get caught in our own steam. Joe's boss is giving him a hard time. Maybe Joe made a mistake or, worse, the boss made the mistake and blamed it on him. In any case, Joe is showing definite signs of a fight-or-flight response. But if he punches out his boss or if he heads for the door muttering, "Take this job and shove it!" chances are he'll be fired. Like many of us, Joe can't find a way to stabilize his nervous system without sacrificing his livelihood. And joblessness is unlikely to decrease anyone's stress levels.

The least destructive way out of this mess is through relaxation. Not only does relaxation help release the steam that builds up inside us every time we're trapped in a fight-or-flight predicament, it can also relieve the headaches, neck cramps, and shoulder pains sustained in our daily pursuit of survival. Relaxation lowers the blood pressure and almost immediately slows the heart rate, decreasing the chances of a heart attack. Over time, lower blood pressure and a slower heart rate add up to more good news:

decelerated aging. That means you won't feel like a sixty-year-old when you're only thirty-five.

If the notions of blood pressure and heart rate are too abstract to understand in the midst of a chaotic day, look at it this way: calming down leads to a better night's sleep. Relaxing before sleep can help you wake up feeling rested. Not unwinding before sleep will leave you tired and stressed out, increasing the wear and tear on your body. And where are you going to live when your body wears out? From this perspective, high stress is tantamount to slow suicide, whereas less stress plus better sleep equals a longer, healthier, and happier life.

Here's the short-range view: relaxation can increase your energy, boost your health, and improve your memory, learning ability, and relationships with other people. Why? Because a calm mind leads to a healthy body, clear thinking, and better social interactions. With less mind fatigue, I find I have more energy to devote to my loved ones and myself. The more attention I give to others and myself, the better I feel. It's also true that when my mind is not clogged up with useless thoughts, it's easier to remember important information and to open myself to new experiences and learning, which enhances peak performance. In this sense, relaxation improves the quality of life.

At this point, you may be wondering, "So if I want a longer, healthier, and happier life, all I have to do is take a walk in the park every day?"

## *The answer is: Yes!*

Before getting to more exercises, let's look at activities you may already be doing because you like them—relaxing pastimes such as walking, reading, or knitting. Do you like to go fishing, or play golf, or binge watch TV? If so, chances are that these hobbies serve as a way for you to relax.

Many people find, for example, that they calm down while out in nature. To some, being in nature means backpacking in the wilderness, whereas to others it means sitting in a lawn chair in the backyard while drinking a beer and turning a nice steak into a piece of charcoal. Maybe for you, being in nature means weeding the vegetables or planting daffodil bulbs. The important point to remember is that whatever helps you relax will also help you feel content. So do more of it. Unless, of course, your relaxing activity is eating chocolate, your pants size has gone from a 32-inch waist to a 38, and the bulk of your disposable income each month goes to the Hershey family. Like my two beers and a cigarette, some activities are relaxing momentarily but ultimately unhealthy. We are looking for healthy, relaxing activities.

A visit to Monument Valley, along the Arizona-Utah border, made me feel wonderful. Maybe it was the sense I had of being a part of something larger than myself; or the vast spaces and massive red sandstone formations I'd seen in old Western movies; or the clean air, blue sky, and huge clouds moving by. The only problem was that I eventually had to return to the workaday world. So what have I done to recapture the serenity I felt there? Every night before going to bed, I kick back and relax by conjuring up the feeling I had in Monument Valley. Now, such an idea may sound like I'm a half-bubble off level, but it works for me. And whatever works for you is the important thing.

I suggest that you find out exactly what helps you relax through your own experience. In the chapters that follow, you will read about a number of ways to relax. Try them all. Some will work for you; some won't. Some you'll like; some you won't. Use the ones that make a difference for you and forget the others. Before long, you're sure to find that you have made life easier on yourself, that you're dictating the circumstances of your life rather than letting them control you.

This is where many books on relaxation fall apart. They ask you to believe in someone else's way of doing things. The first relaxation books I read were from the Far East. Lavishly illustrated, they showed people with shaved heads and saffron robes, and came wrapped with incense or photos of Tibetan monks chanting with a bell choir. For a while I was afraid I'd never learn to relax, because incense made me sneeze and I wasn't accustomed to being ceremonial, nor could I sit in the recommended cross-legged lotus position for hours at a time. One book said I must be able to sit quietly for forty-five minutes twice a day or I would receive no benefit from the program. If I could sit quietly for forty-five minutes I wouldn't need this guy's program.

One book did say, "East Indian forms of relaxation often are not suitable for Westerners. The technique a person uses must be compatible with their own culture."

I had let my own culture make me berserk. As I've described, my blood pressure was up, my pulse was 10% over normal (normal for me, that is), and my breathing was so shallow it was hardly noticeable.

But those words were good news to me and helped me understand that I didn't have to become a Hindu or a Buddhist or a yogi to learn to relax, and neither do you.

Mark Twain once said, "I don't need anyone to tell me what to do. I already don't do half the things I know I should do."

The only question is, what are you willing to do? The next few pages will show you the simple, easy things I did to learn to calm down. If I can do it, so can you. Just try a couple of the exercises. Most of them are actually fun. I know you'll find at least one you like and that you are willing to do regularly. Most importantly, enjoy!

# 3

# Countdown to Peace and Quiet

When my mom's life wasn't going her way, she would say, "That person or situation aggravates me." Then her voice would inch up a little higher, her words would tumble out a bit faster, and a hint of hysteria would creep in. While watching her get annoyed on the outside and miserable on the inside, I would think, "Mom, calm down." But saying those words to her would have been like telling my dog Cookie not to dig in the backyard...useless. Worry and agitation were ingrained in Mom's nature.

Oddly enough, my mother often told me to have patience. "I don't have it," she would admit. "I've never been a patient person, but you should be."

"How can I do that?" I'd ask.

"Count to ten," she'd always say.

Because she never counted to ten, I was always baffled by the "Do as I say, not as I do" message. Usually, I forgot to count and as a result I was miserable. But sometimes I did count to ten, and occasionally it worked.

As an adult searching for ways to quiet the mind chatter going on inside of me, I discovered that all the mind needed was something to keep it busy. Then I arrived at an exercise that worked more often than it didn't. And sure enough, it was a mind-absorbing variation on counting to ten.

## EXERCISE II

# Counting Backwards to Quiet the Mind

Here you are going to count backwards from fifteen to zero with your eyes closed. Read through the instructions first so you'll know what to do. This exercise will take less than one minute.

» Sit comfortably and close your eyes. Then take three slow breaths to calm down and clear your mind.

» Breathing easily, inhale. Now exhale, silently saying, "Fifteen."

» Inhale again. This time while exhaling, silently say, "Fourteen."

» Continue inhaling and counting down one number with each exhale.

» After you reach zero, take a few gentle breaths, all the while noticing how you feel. When you are ready, open your eyes.

Were the results better than those of the Not Thinking exercise? Were there fewer random thoughts clogging up your mind? Most people find it easier to count down than to try to stop thinking. Why? Because the mind is more reined in when it has a task to perform.

Counting is a simple task, and paying attention to the task at hand will bring us into the present moment, the Here & Now. Yogi Berra, the famed New York Yankees catcher and manager, understood this principle and once said, "How can you think and hit at the same time?"

Yes, while counting backward, the mind can drift off to other thoughts, as you may have found, but it will come quickly back to the business at hand. Better yet, while concentrating on this task, you cannot also be thinking about people or situations that aggravate or annoy you. As a result, you will be more relaxed. Vary this exercise by changing the numbers, counting down from eighteen to three, for example, or from thirty-three to sixteen. This will help keep your mind occupied.

Relaxation happens between thoughts. But with 60,000 thoughts a day, most of which consist of mind chatter, we don't have much time left over for relaxation. To pave the way for more down time, we must clear the mind of the chatter.

As you may have already experienced, clearing the mind is not as easy as it sounds. For example, while counting backward, did you start to fall asleep? Many people do. It's like sitting down to an unpleasant task and becoming drowsy as soon as you begin. Your next thought is "Let me take a nap, then I'll be up to this." The problem in both instances is that the mind would rather go to sleep than engage in a difficult task. When faced with a simple task, however, the mind does not want to let go of thinking, even for a minute. The solution? Concentrate sharply on the counting, and you won't fall asleep.

Here's another mind trick: by the end of the exercise, were you counting backward and thinking at the same time? This maneuver is similar to what happens after learning to drive a car. At first, it takes all our concentration to put the car in drive, ease down on the gas pedal and drive a short distance; a year later, we can burn up the highway hardly thinking about the fact that we're driving. By then, the mind has conquered driving so completely that it wants to do something else...such as think! It wants to rewrite the outcomes of yesterday's scenarios or strategize for tomorrow.

When I started practicing relaxation, I preferred an agitated state of mind to a calm one. Being agitated was comforting because it's what I was used to. I wanted to stay pissed off at people who annoyed me. But with a little more experience in relaxation, I discovered how much it paid off provided I have the willingness to practice and the courage to change old habits.

What I found was that clearing the mind is like exercising a muscle: the more you work it, the stronger it gets.

With practice, your mind drifts off less frequently, stays away for shorter periods of time, and comes back more easily. For now, simply notice when your mind has strayed off and bring it back to counting.

Years ago, Harvard University Medical School published a report stating that counting backward lowers a person's blood pressure and heart rate. This means that if you're agitated and begin breathing a little deeper, counting down from fifteen with each exhale, you will instantly let off steam and calm down. If you don't have time for the countdown, at least stop and take the three slow breaths.

Practice both of these relaxation techniques day and night, preferably when you're not angry. That way, any time you start to get upset, you'll soon be able to achieve the state of mind my mom could only talk about. The three slow breaths will calm you down in less than ten seconds. Counting backward from fifteen to zero will relieve even more layers of stress in less than sixty seconds.

## POINTS TO REMEMBER

Your mind loves to think.

If you give your mind a task to carry out,
it will quiet down—at least for a while.

Once your mind has learned the task,
it will give it back to you to do and will go on thinking.

To strengthen your mind's ability
to clear itself of chatter,
practice breathing and counting backward.

### PART TWO

# Finding a Point of Focus

# 4

# Your Mind
# Thinks It's You

Now that you know how to calm down, let's go a little deeper. When I started to practice holding a point of focus, I felt a deeper calm and more self-confidence. As you work with these exercises—or at least the ones you like most–you will not only quiet your mind in the moment, but also begin to experience an inner peace and an easier life. These are the lasting effects of relaxation.

Let's start by looking at the mind. My mind, scattered and full of thoughts, resembles a wild horse. Attempting to concentrate on something is like trying to tame that horse; if you approach it with anything as confining as a saddle, it will probably run away. The mind is tricky. It flees from constraints. It learns new tasks, teaches them to me, and then goes about its business of thinking other thoughts. In short, it does what it wants to do.

Your mind probably does, too. Your seat of intelligence and reason fancies itself not only in charge of your thinking, but the beginning and end of everything you say and do.

*In other words, your mind thinks it's you.*

You are not your mind nor is it you. Also, your thoughts are not you. Remember the very first exercise, Three Slow Breaths; for ten seconds you were concentrating on your breath, not thinking about your kids, partner, or the day you will die. Nor is our nervousness, our anxiety, or our emotions in general the real you.

Contrary to your mind's highfalutin' notions, however, there's more to us than this ticker tape of thinking. If we occupy our mind with a task and slip past it, other parts of us such as our instinct and intuition will rise to the surface.

Athletes call that being in the Zone when they don't think, but let their body take over. A good golfer will swing the club and send his tee shot straight down the fairway without thinking through each segment of his swing. He's confident that his body instinctively knows how to hit the ball once he has decided what he wants the ball to do. With the mind out of the way, golf can be enormously relaxing, but with the mind choreographing each stroke, golf can be stressful enough to cause a heart attack. The outcome depends on how we approach the game, and on how we approach our lives.

Let's talk about our intuition. It is something that comes from deep inside of us. It is deeper than our mind, our thoughts, and emotions. That is our final destination, a place in us that is not touched, not influenced by the outside world. We will get there, slowly, but the first step is you remembering your own intuition. Intuition bubbles up like a little voice in our ear when we start listening to our heart or our gut. Maybe it's a sensation in our bodies that can be the reception of our intuition. Think of it as a sixth sense that overrides logical solutions, which somehow you know won't solve the problem at hand. When we quiet our mind, then clearly and more often we hear the voice of intuition.

There are vibrations, maybe a sensation in our bodies that can be the reception of our intuition. Some people say they hear their intuition. Joan of Arc and the Son of Sam both said they heard voices. Can you tell the difference between the voice of God and your neighbor's dog? Right. Be careful; hearing voices is not foolproof, and it can get us into a lot of trouble.

Here's an example—listen to the voice that comes up when you've just made a mistake—the one that tells you how stupid you are. Got that one? That's not the voice I'm talking about. That is NOT the voice of your intuition.

Personally, I have many voices in my head—my ex-wife, my mother, and my last boss. And believe me—I don't listen to any of those voices.

To hear the voice of my intuition, I must be in the present moment, the *Here & Now*. Sometimes something grabs our attention; we aren't trying, it just happens.

Let's take an example of a moment in your life when you were completely paying attention to what was happening and you did hear the voice of your intuition.

Remember back to a time when you went on a blind date or a first date. There were introductions and maybe some small talk, but within the first few minutes you knew this was NOT the person for you. How did you know? You were totally engaged in the moment. Call it intuition or instinct. Call it in the Zone, but you knew.

Then what happens to a lot of us is that our thinking mind decides it knows better than our intuition and begins talking us out of listening to the message we have received. When we fail to listen to our intuition and intuitive messages, there can be dire consequences.

How many of us had to go back for a second date just to prove to our thinking mind that this was NOT the person for us?

Some of us have even more stubborn minds. Some people actually have to marry that person to prove they aren't the right one for us.

Listen to the voice that comes to you in the gap between your thoughts, whether your eyes are open or you're sitting quietly. Don't listen to all of the voices that rattle around in your head.

The key to hearing or receiving our intuition–gut feeling is staying in the Present Moment, the Here & Now.

To get your mind out of the way enough to follow your instinct or hear the voice of intuition, you don't need to harness it; just give it a single point of focus. Each of the exercises in the next few chapters will teach you to hold one point of focus—such as one picture in your mind's eye, one sound in your mind's ear—and stay with it. Any time your mind drifts away from the single point you've chosen, and you begin to notice a different thought unfolding into an entire TV miniseries, you will have this point to come back to, something to refocus on. With practice, you are able to achieve what you want at will...quite literally, a little peace of mind.

Here are two final thoughts to consider before trying to get rid of your mind chatter. First, approach each exercise as an experiment. My job is to find the one technique/exercise that suits you as an individual. This is for you. So, start with something to which you can relate. You must begin where you are. That's why I suggest you choose a technique that suits your temperament. The fact is that you may not like all these techniques or even half of them. If you like one, however, then that's the one for you.

Second, no matter how out of control your everyday world may be, don't expect it to vanish. We see the results of practice in our daily life, in our relationships and our tolerance of others.

Similarly, the purpose of practicing these point-of-focus exercises is not to hide from life. On the contrary, practicing them will bring us more into our life so that we can live our lives fully.

# 5

# Wheel of Life

One year on vacation, my wife and I were driving down a road in southern New Hampshire when we came upon an "Antiques" sign that directed us by way of a large red arrow down a dirt road. The tree-lined lane led to an old barn that had been converted into a store. Inside the store, I found a wagon wheel, its painted hub looking much like the sun. I couldn't tell if the sun was rising or setting, if it signified the beginning or end of the day, which, I suppose, was the point. Painted on each spoke of the wheel was a word or a phrase: "Family," "Right Livelihood," "Homestead," "Service to Others," "Unity of Humankind." Stepping back, I realized that the wagon wheel portrayed the facets of a person's life.

To this day, I can close my eyes and see that wagon wheel, right down to the words on its spokes. I think of it as the wheel of my life. There am I, Fred, in the middle. My sun is both rising and setting. As I contemplate the spokes, I can almost see how I'm doing in each area of my life. What's more, every spoke shows me how important all the others are if I am to move forward. Balance is essential or the wheel won't turn.

Whenever I concentrate on the wheel of my life, it becomes my sole point of focus and carries me into a state of deep relaxation. Although the wheel itself is no longer in my environment, it is in my mind's eye, where it remains eternally available to me. When I visualize it, I become immediately calm and reflective.

# 6

# Touch, Scent, and Taste

Feeling, smelling, and tasting are strong, immediate senses. We'll begin holding one point of focus by working with each of them. Why?

*Because for us human beings, it is nearly impossible not to think. But we can choose what we think about.*

Each of the following exercises gives us the opportunity to exercise our muscle of concentration. The ability to concentrate deeply will pay dividends in all areas of our lives, as you will see as we progress through this book.

## One Point of Touching

During one of the many times I tried to quit smoking, someone gave me a small, flat stone. "Treat it like Greek worry beads," he advised me. "When you want a cigarette, rub the stone." In the short run, it worked. Many times, when I was thinking about having a cigarette, I would take the stone out of my pocket and hold it, look at it, then turn it over and over in my hand. After I'd spent a few seconds holding the stone, the urge for a cigarette would pass. Why? Because I couldn't think about the stone and a cigarette at the same time.

In the long run, I started smoking again, since there's more to staying off cigarettes than merely taking your mind off them for a few seconds at a time. In the longer run, however, I quit for good. Even so, I still carry a small stone with me. Every time I reach into my pocket for change, the stone is there to remind me that I can clear my mind by holding it. If I'm feeling nervous or annoyed, into my pocket I go to stop the rumbling in my head.

Connecting tactilely to an object by touching it may be the easiest point of concentration we have. Because the sense of touch is so engaging and convincing, it has been incorporated into a variety of devotional rituals. People of many different religions, for example, hold strings of beads and, while touching each one, recite a designated prayer to go with it.

To experiment with touch as a point of focus, try the one below. First, you'll need to select an object from your surroundings, such as a lucky charm, a talisman, or a small stone.

## EXERCISE III

# Touching an Object

» Sit quietly, holding your chosen object, and take three slow breaths.
» Close your eyes. Concentrate on the object in your hand.
» Whenever you notice your thoughts starting to drift off, squeeze or rub the object to bring your attention back to it.
» When you are ready, take a few deep breaths and open your eyes.

If your object is small, try carrying it around with you and practicing this exercise spontaneously. A larger object can be left at home in plain sight to serve as a reminder to keep practicing.

## One Point of Smelling

For many people, scent ushers in the strongest sensory impressions. Until recently, I was not one of these people. In fact, I couldn't remember a smell at all until a teacher asked me to describe my grandmother's kitchen. Right away, I recalled the aroma of fresh cornbread. Next, I could see it cooling in a covered cast-iron skillet on the stove.

What did your grandmother's kitchen smell like? Baked casseroles, fresh pies, spices? Or how about a favorite aunt's kitchen, or a best friend's? If you've never spent much time in kitchens, try to recall the perfume or cologne worn by your last date or a special person in your life. Somewhere, there is a fragrance you once loved, and right now you can smell it. Scent evokes powerful memories.

To work with smell as a point of focus, try the next one. It will help you concentrate on aromas in your immediate environment that may soon become calming memories in your mind. Before beginning this exercise, scan the room for a delectable scent, or set a bouquet of flowers nearby to serve as your point of focus. If you need something stronger, light a scented candle or burn a stick of incense.

**EXERCISE IV**

# Tuning into Smell

» Sit quietly and comfortably and take three slow breaths.
» Closing your eyes, concentrate on your chosen aroma.
» Briefly, let your mind run wild with thoughts. Between thoughts, let your mind come back to the aroma.
» Now begin to focus only on the aroma. Any time you notice yourself drifting into thinking, direct your concentration back to the scent, your one point of focus.
» When you are ready, take some deeper slow breaths and open your eyes.

After just a few minutes of concentrating on a smell, you are likely to find that your thoughts have slowed down and your mind is a little quieter. If so, your sense of smell may be highly developed, in which case you'll want to keep aroma in mind whenever you feel the need to calm down.

# One Point of Tasting

Have you ever seen a plate of food arranged so attractively you could almost taste it? Have you ever smelled an aroma so strongly you thought you could taste it, such as garlic roasting in olive oil or salt in the sea air at low tide?

Taste, a captivating sense, is able to gain our attention through sight and smell even before our taste buds are engaged. Once they do connect with a morsel of any sort, the sensation of taste is relatively short-lived, unless it's sustained through touch and smell. For example, how often have you felt the first soothing rush of flavor from a breath mint only to forget about it seconds later? Many of us disregard that mint in our mouth until we've crunched the last speck of hardness between our back teeth.

What happened between the first burst of flavor and that last crunch? We lost conscious contact with the mint because we stopped concentrating on it! Had we touched it with our tongue and smelled its aroma wafting up from our mouths, we could have prolonged the taste experience and the calmness it awakened.

The next exercise will help you give the sense of taste your full attention. This time the prop you will need is a *LifeSaver*—either red, green, yellow, orange, or white, whichever is your favorite. If you don't like *LifeSavers*, use the mint of your choice.

**EXERCISE V**

# Taste: A Veritable Lifesaver

» Sit comfortably and take three slow breaths. Then pop the *LifeSaver* into your mouth.

» As best you can, focus on the taste of the candy: the cherry, lime, lemon, orange, or pineapple flavor.

» While concentrating on the taste, resist the temptation to chew. (Sucking the candy can result in a longer period of focused attention, so see if you can keep it going that way.)

» When the *LifeSaver* has fully dissolved, notice how much fun you've had calming down.

# 7

# Sound and Sight

If you are accustomed to using your ears and eyes, then these organs of perception are already fine-tuned enough to focus on one point. Your ears are well-trained in concentrating on sound. Similarly, your eyes have been sending messages to your brain for years. It's just a small jump to go from hearing or seeing to a deepened state of relaxation.

## One Point of Hearing

One summer I lived in a beach house nearly at the water's edge. Each night, I could hear the surf breaking lightly on the sand. The more I listened to it, the more I relaxed. Come fall, I returned to city life, where the sound of the waves was replaced by the noise of sirens and car horns.

If you're lucky enough to be living in a beach house year-round, or to have a babbling brook in your backyard, or be within walking distance of a perpetual waterfall, you can close your eyes and endlessly take in the soothing sound of moving water. But if your only source of continuously running water is your toilet, you'd be better off downloading a few tracks of environmental sounds. If a summer rainstorm brings back memories of the best days of your childhood, then that's the sound for you. Soothing music is another possibility, especially arrangements that let you concentrate on one note at a time.

Whichever option you've decided on, prepare to make sound the one point you focus on, the one point you come back to. Begin by turning on your sound and trying the following exercise.

## EXERCISE VI

# Relaxing to Sound

» Sit quietly and comfortably, and take three slow breaths.
» For a few minutes, let your mind run wild with whatever thoughts come up.
» Now close your eyes and begin to focus on your sound.
» Any time you notice that you have drifted into thinking, bring your concentration back to your sound. Shifting your focus back to your sound will be calming, and pleasant, and you are exercising your concentration.
» Spend as much time as you like listening to your sound. When you're finished, take a few slow breaths and open your eyes.

## One Point of Seeing

The next exercise will help you move from merely seeing a point of focus to truly visualizing it. This is a two-part exercise: Part 1 involves staring open-eyed at an object, and Part 2 entails closing your eyes and recreating in your mind's eye an image of that object. The object can be anything you choose. Look around the room and pick something. The exercise refers to a candle, although your object can just as well be a picture of your family, a flower arrangement, an icon, or anything else you enjoy looking at. If you like the idea of a candle, anything from a dinner candle to a birthday candle will do. Just set it on a table and light it.

## EXERCISE VII

# First Seeing,
# Then Introduction to Visualizing

### Part 1

Sit back and take three slow breaths. Begin to breathe gently, and as you do, watch the flicker of the candle flame. When you become distracted by a thought, try to "watch" the thought go by as if watching a bus rather than jumping on the bus and going for a ride. As the thought passes, bring your attention back to the flame.

For a few seconds, keep your concentration on the candle flame, your one point of focus.

### Part 2

When visualizing, some people see sharp, vivid color pictures–images. Others see somewhat fuzzy–grainy, black and white images. Still others never see an image at all but have a sense or a feeling of the image or object. Don't expect too much from this exercise. It is more about you connecting with the essence of the object, what the image represents to you.

For example, a photo of your family or a group reunion may have more emotional connection than a beautiful but random landscape. A religious icon that is near and dear to you will have a deeper meaning than a garage sale knickknack.

For a few seconds, keep your concentration on the candle flame, your one point of focus.

Then close your eyes and see the image of the flame—not behind your eyelids, but in your mind's eye, the place in your head where thoughts play out like movies.

Hold your concentration on the image of the flame. Any time you notice that your mind has drifted away from this image, invite it to come back. Do not be harsh with yourself or judge your ability. Your mind will drift—there's no way around this phenomenon, as you well know, but continue to exercise your muscle of concentration.

While practicing visualizing, you may have to work with Part 1—Seeing—for a while before achieving even small success with Part 2—visualizing—an object. Remember, many people never see an image at all, but some have a sense or feel of their object. I can't explain this, but it is more likely to happen with an object that has an emotional connection, like a family photo, spiritual/religious icon, etc. If you never do see an image, don't worry. This exercise is not for you but there are many others to try. If and when you do move fully into visualizing, don't be surprised if the image changes after you close your eyes. In your mind's eye, a candle flame can become a full moon, a sunrise, or any number of other sights. Let whatever happens happen... then stay with it as long as you can.

Staring open-eyed at a candle flame is a centuries-old concentration practice. A more recent one has practitioners looking into a mirror for minutes at a time. This approach is said to awaken insight into oneself. Whichever point of focus you most enjoy working with, exercise your concentration muscle often, though not necessarily for extended periods of time. This technique will get easier with practice and a set routine. That's a promise.

# 8

# Head Movies

Did you ever want to make a movie? Movies in your head, sometimes called visualizations, provide a sure-fire way to calm down during a coffee break or chill after a ghastly day.

Remember how I relax by imagining myself back in Monument Valley? Well, you can immerse yourself in the same sort of experience by taking a trip to the beach. Join me on this two-minute excursion and then create a "vacation getaway" of your own.

Remember what I said in the last chapter regarding visualizations. When visualizing, some people see sharp, vivid color pictures or images. Others see somewhat fuzzy-grainy, black and white images. Still others never see an image at all but have a sense or a feeling of the image or object. Don't expect too much from this exercise. It is more about you connecting with the essence of the object—what the image represents to you.

Also, this exercise is a trip to the beach. Maybe you have never been to the beach and don't want to go. Pick anywhere in nature you like or would like to visit. Take your mind to a forest, the desert, or a mountain meadow. It makes no difference whether you go to a place you've been to before or one you've dreamed about. What matters is that you remember to use all your senses.

## EXERCISE VIII

# A Trip to the Beach

» Read through this exercise once, then go back and talk yourself through it.

» Pull the lever on your recliner, close your eyes, and take three slow breaths.

» Imagine yourself sitting at the seashore. See the blue sky, the blue-green water, and the clouds overhead.

» Watch the waves as they roll in, break, and recede. Get into the easy, gentle rhythm of the waves.

» See the white sand around you. Feel it.

» Now feel the warm sun on your arms and shoulders.

» Feel a cool breeze touch your face.

» Smell the sea air.

» Smile. Let this pleasant scene relax you.

» Taste the salt in the air.

» Listen to the waves as they break against the shore and roll back out again.

» Hear a seagull cry in the distance.

The more of your senses you call into action, the more this beach scene will calm you down. Why? Because your mind will be fully absorbed in the head movie, focused on seeing, feeling, smelling, tasting, and hearing the real world you have created.

Next time you need to chill, close your eyes, take three slow breaths, and imagine yourself anywhere in nature; using all your senses, see, feel, smell, taste, and hear the ocean.

Head movies can be a special treat at bedtime. The next exercises will help you drift peacefully off to sleep.

# 9

# As You Think, So You Feel

## Here you can see the power of your thoughts in action.

————————◆————————

### EXERCISE IX

Read this exercise slowly before trying it.

Sit back, close your eyes, take three slow breaths, and think about something that makes you happy. Be specific, such as a hobby, your partner, chocolate, or your pet. I have a little black cat named Scruffy. Every time I think about her, it makes me smile.

If you know how to take your pulse at your wrist or the side of your neck, do so. Or, simply notice how good you feel.

Next, to change your feelings, see in your mind's eye a place you dread, such as your office or the dentist, a classroom or a courtroom.

Slowly approach the building. As you do, feel your discomfort increasing. Your heart rate may pick up, or tension may creep into your neck and shoulders.

Keep watching as you open the door. See your boss, the judge, or whoever the biggest "pain in the neck" may be in this scene. Can you feel your jaw muscles tightening or your hands trembling ever so slightly? Take your pulse once again. Is it faster this time?

Before doing anything else, take three slow breaths.
Go back to thinking about what makes you happy.

At this point, you should be feeling better. Moreover, you now have proof that you can take action to change your thinking, and that changing your thinking will alter how you feel. Think fearful thoughts, and your stress level will rise; use Head Movies to concentrate on pleasant thoughts, and it will drop.

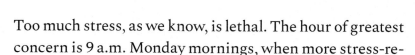

Too much stress, as we know, is lethal. The hour of greatest concern is 9 a.m. Monday mornings, when more stress-related deaths occur than at any other time of the week. This means that if you regularly begin your week in a setting that puts a crick in your neck, you would be wise to tune into a Head Movie. Relax first thing on Monday morning, and you'll lessen your chances of imminent illness, injury, or death.

But don't wait until Monday morning. Many people get the Sunday night blahs just thinking about the next day. If you do, too, create a movie in your head to reframe the situation at work. See things going pleasantly for you the next day. See yourself getting along well with the boss, your coworkers, and clients. See how well you can get along with the person who's been a pain the neck. In short, create a Head Movie that helps you have a better working situation on the job.

With practice, these exercises will become easier to use. Then the more you use them, the more they will enhance your life.

# 10

## Living Breath

Breath is a handy point of focus because it is with us constantly. In fact, we can't possibly leave home without it. Besides, it's been around a long time; even before we had our first taste of milk, we experienced our breath. Because breathing has been such a loyal companion throughout our lives, we tend to think we know it well.

Think again! Since we've started most of the previous exercises by taking three slow breaths, you already know how soothing that can be. But there may be aspects of breathing you have never thought about. The exercises that follow can be used to engage your mind in some of these subtler experiences. Never again will you be able to take breathing for granted!

---

## EXERCISE X

# The Touch of Breath

While doing this exercise, keep your eyes open, keep reading, and keep breathing.

Breathing easily, notice where the air enters and leaves your nostrils. In each instance you will be able to feel the spot where your breath first touches the inside of your nose. (If you can't breathe through your nose, separate your lips ever so slightly and feel where your breath touches them.)

Continue to concentrate on your nostrils. Don't follow the air down into your throat and lungs; pay no attention to how cold or warm the air is; disregard any odors you may notice. Just concentrate on the sensual, tactile feeling of friction that arises as the air brushes across the skin inside your nostrils while entering and leaving your nose.

If you suddenly become conscious of the movement of your chest, bring your attention back to where the air is entering and leaving your nostrils. Feel it as it passes in and out...in and out.

Become absorbed in the air entering and leaving your nostrils. Observe but don't judge whether your breaths are short or long. Continue breathing in and out...in and out.

If your mind wanders, don't feel guilty. Just allow it to come back to where the air is entering and leaving your nostrils.

Now notice there are actually FOUR parts to each full breath. After you inhale, when your lungs have filled with air, there is a very slight transition, a pause, then comes the exhale, followed by a pause, then the next inhale. Continue breathing in and out...in and out.

Do you sometimes "miss" the inhale or the exhale because your mind has wandered away? How about one of the pauses? If so, recognize that you were distracted and allow your mind to come back to the spot where you can feel the air entering and leaving your nostrils.

After a while, observe your mind. Have your thoughts slowed down? Has a feeling of serenity begun to permeate your inner being?

That breath exercise will give you a point of focus as well as a sense of deep relaxation wherever you happen to be. Try it while visiting a friend in the hospital or while waiting to board a flight that's been delayed for two hours. Any time you can't escape for a few minutes of peace and quiet, much less go for a walk in the woods, stop what you are doing and concentrate only on the breath in your nostrils.

There's no need for explanations since no one around you will know what you are doing! You can do these breathing exercises with your eyes wide open, sitting at your desk or a red light.

The next two exercises can be done with your eyes either open or closed. If you are in public, consider keeping your eyes open. If you are at home, close them; that will deepen the experience for you.

## EXERCISE XI

# Warming the Air You Breathe

» Sit quietly and take three slow breaths.

» Now breathe normally, feeling the breath in your nostrils as you did in Exercise X.

» Now notice the temperature of your breath as it enters and leaves through your nose. The outside air will feel cool upon entering your nostrils and the exhale slightly warmer as it leaves your lungs.

» Continue to concentrate on the temperature of your breath.

» After a few minutes, observe that you are still concentrating on the temperature of your breath, and not on thinking.

Here's another possibility: breathe through your nose and listen to the sound your breath makes. If at first you can't hear it, take slightly stronger and deeper breaths, then listen for the sound inside your head. On the inhale, the breath inside your head will sound like So; on the exhale, it will sound like Hum. With a full breath, you will hear So-Hum. Think of it as the silent whisper of your breath.

Isn't it curious that your breath has been repeating the word-sounds So-Hum to you 35,000 times a day since the moment you were born and you never knew it? Well, the good news is that now you do know it and can tune into this silent whisper any time you want to. Better yet, it happens all by itself, with no effort on your part, as you will see in the following exercise.

## EXERCISE XII

# The Soothing Voice in Your Head

This point of focus exercise can quickly lead you into a state of deep relaxation.

» Sit comfortably and take three slow breaths.

» Breathing normally, pay attention to the So sound your breath makes as you inhale.

» While exhaling, hear the Hum sound.

» Continue to concentrate on the So–Hum of your breath, listening quietly and calmly to this soothing voice in your head.

» After a few minutes, notice how much more relaxing this voice is than any other voice you may hear in your head.

All three of these breath exercises will help you reach a new level of calm. As you practice your favorite one, peacefulness will sink into you more deeply than before, and it will last longer. Luxuriate in this peacefulness. Hang out with it—take it to the laundromat or the library. Treat it well, because within it lie the seeds of self-confidence and a more positive attitude toward life.

# 11

# Welcoming Words

One day, when I was about fourteen years old, my mother gave me a wallet card embossed with the Serenity Prayer. She told me that when I got aggravated, I should repeat this prayer; it would calm me down. By then I had learned how to keep peace with my mother. Taking the card, I put it in my wallet, and the next day I threw it away. One of the things that aggravated me the most, as a teenager, was being told what to do.

### THE SERENITY PRAYER *

God, grant me the serenity to
accept the things I cannot change,
the courage to change the things I can,
and the wisdom to know the difference.

(© 1962 Reinhold Niebuhr—American theologian 1892-1971)

For many of us, childhood had religious overtones. Some of us were given a string of beads and prayers to say over and over again for each bead, as in the Catholic and Hindu faiths. Others thumbed through books of scriptures, repeating prayers, as in the Jewish and Buddhist traditions. Whatever your childhood exposures were like, repeating prayers at this stage in your life could well become a form of relaxation. If you enjoy and do it because you want to, it may even lead to a mystical experience.

But if you, like me, did not enjoy repeating prayers, it can feel like a penance.

The practice of repeating words to calm down the emotions has been around for as long as there have been words to repeat. Its calming effect comes from using words and their meaning as a point of focus.

What set of words, if any, do you like to say over and over? What words bring you joy and guidance? Maybe it is a prayer from your youth or perhaps a new one to you.

My friend Marcia is not religious, but she is still partial to the 46th Psalm—"Be Still and Know that I Am God." Also, the Serenity Prayer is a good one. Or how about one of these...

## PRAYER OF ST. FRANCIS OF ASSISI (Peace Prayer)

Lord, make me an instrument of Thy peace;
where there is hatred, let me sow love;
where there is injury, pardon;
where there is doubt, faith;
where there is despair, hope;
where there is darkness, light;
and where there is sadness, joy.

O Divine Master,
grant that I may not so much
seek to be consoled, as to console;
to be understood, as to understand;
to be loved, as to love;
for it is in giving that we receive,
it is in pardoning that we are pardoned,
and it is in dying that we are born to eternal life.

### Shema

She-ma Yis-ra-el    *(Hear, O Israel)*
A-do-noi El-o-ha-nu    *(the Lord our God)*
A-do-noi Eeh-had    *(the Lord is One)*

Or recite a favorite poem, such as Robert Frost's "Stopping by Woods on a Snowy Evening," which ends with a repetition of the line "And miles to go before I sleep." If you like to sing, begin chanting your most loved spiritual song, such as "Amazing Grace," which begins with the inspiring words "Amazing grace, how sweet the sound that saved a wretch like me!" Even if your favorite song is Janis Joplin singing "Oh Lord, won't you buy me a Mercedes Benz," that is the one for you. When deciding on a poem or song to use as a point of focus, be sure to choose one that touches you. Then see what it does for your mind.

Whatever song, poem, or prayer you decide on, write it down and read it until you have it memorized. Then recite it each time you feel the steam of anxiety rising inside you.

Here is a technique I picked up along my journey that incorporates words and your breath. Let's say you chose Psalm 46:10 to quiet your mind. Silently repeat the words as you inhale and exhale.

"Be Still and Know that I Am God"

Next, for a couple of breaths, break the words in half
for inhale and exhale.

Inhale—Be Still and Know
Exhale—that I Am God

Then, drop one word and use a
shorter breath a few times.

Inhale—Be Still
Exhale—Know God

Finally, relax your breath completely
and let your body breathe.

Silently
Inhale—Know
Exhale—God

If you chose *Amazing Grace*, the final words might be,
Grace—Found. Or from…Woods on a Snowy Evening,
Promises—Keep.

Remember, the techniques that suit the teacher may not
suit the student, so don't be turned away by these exam-
ples. Use the words that quiet your mind, sooth your heart,
and stir your soul. Those are the words that will work the
best for you.

# 12

## Sleep

Just try getting to sleep after a stressful day. If your mind is stressed, your body is too. What is worse than that? Getting a little sleep, waking up, then trying to get back to sleep. Do you have trouble getting to sleep or back to sleep in the middle of the night?

There are dozens of possible factors to consider in how to get a good night's sleep. Here are only a few, but worthwhile thinking about.

What you eat and when you eat it. Use common sense. Late dinners are not good for your waistline or for sleep. Spicy food, even if it doesn't give you indigestion, stimulates your system.

Exercise in the morning. Do anything that you like to do. In the evening, don't build up your energy; instead, quiet down. Try a gentle evening walk or some mild relaxing stretches. A breathing exercise can and will relax both your mind and your body. Try one that you like from the Living Breath chapter.

The last hour before bed is crucial. Don't feed your mind junk food. Put down the cell phone, tablet, and computer. Scientist are now telling us Blue Light from screens is ruining our sleep. Turn off the television to avoid late evening news shows and violent dramas. They agitate the mind and cause endless "mind chatter" through the night. Reading helps many people, but on paper, not on a screen.

Next comes our own body clock and energy cycle. Eastern medicine tells us a lighter, airier energy dominates from 2 to 6 in the morning and afternoon, a heavier, earthier energy from 6 to 10 morning and night, and a hotter, livelier energy from 10 a.m. till 2 p.m. and again from 10 p.m. until 2 a.m. What does that mean to us? Try to get to bed by 10 p.m. before you get that second wind of livelier energy that will keep you up. Also, be up by 6 a.m. before the heavy energy kicks in and glues you to the bed. I know, I know, when I say this to people they either already do it or they never will. If you already do, stick with it. If you never have, give it a try and see if it works for you. If you never will, the next best thing is a consistent sleep schedule. Go to bed and get up about the same time every day, at least Monday through Friday.

Now, as time permits, continue your nightly routine in the order you prefer. Change into your nightclothes, wash your hands and face, brush your teeth, and all of the other things you do. Moving slowly, winding down to allow your mind and body to begin to relax.

Try using a sleep mask because light stimulates brain activity. After you are in bed with the lights out, relax your body and mind.

### TOES TO NOSE

Lie on your back.
Take three slow breaths and feel your gentle breathing.

*Surrender to gravity.*

Feel your heels on the mattress.
Relax your feet and ankles.

Feel your calves and back of your thighs
on the mattress. Relax them.

Feel your buttocks and low back on the mattress.

Relax there and as you exhale, relax your low belly.

Feel your arms, hands, and fingers
on the mattress. Relax them.

Feel your back on the mattress.

As you exhale, relax your chest and back.

Relax your shoulders.

Feel the back of your head on the pillow.

Swallow, relaxing your throat and neck.

Relax your jaw muscles and release your
tongue from the roof of your mouth.

Feel your gentle breathing in your nostrils.

**To calm the static between the ears, create a
Head Movie to quiet the mind chatter.**

## EXERCISE XIII

# A Walk in the Woods

This visualization is best performed with your eyes closed, so read through it once before trying it. Use it not only to help you fall asleep but also to assist you in getting back to sleep when you have awakened during the night.

» With your eyes closed, take three slow breaths, and imagine yourself walking along a path in the woods. See the brown bark of the trees, smell their green leaves. Feel the warm sun on your back. Hear the birds chirping.

» Walking deeper into the woods, see the blue sky and white clouds. Feel a cool breeze on your cheeks and the softness of the ground under your feet.

» Walking deeper and deeper into the woods, listen to a twig snap underfoot and really hear it.

» As you round a bend, notice a cabin nestled among the trees. See wisps of smoke floating out of the chimney. Smell the fragrant wood burning in the fireplace. This is your cabin.

» Approach the cabin, open the door, and step inside. The fireplace on the far wall is crackling with golden-orange flames. In front of it is a thick rug, and folded up at one end of this rug is your favorite blanket and pillow.

» Close the door behind you and walk over to the fire-place. Warm your body, front and back. Stretch out on the rug, feeling very comfortable, safe, and contented. Covering yourself with the blanket, drift off to a peaceful sleep.

One last thing. Sometimes no matter how much I relax my body, when all is said and done, my mind is still too active to let me sleep. In other words, my world is quiet but I can't stop thinking.

*Remember, for us human beings it is nearly impossible not to think. But we can choose what we think about.*

If this is your situation also, don't let your mind run wild; choose what you want to think about. I use a combination of Welcoming Words and Living Breath. Again, here is the place where you must choose an affirmation, song, poem, or prayer to quiet your mind. No matter which example I give, I'm sure to offend someone.

I am returning to "Amazing Grace" and the line I choose is "And Grace will lead me Home." After you have worked your way from your toes to your nose or have stretched out in front of the fire in your cabin, silently say as you:

Inhale—And Grace will lead me Home
Exhale—And Grace will lead me Home

Three times—then

Inhale—And Grace will
Exhale—lead me Home

Three times—then

Inhale—Grace
Exhale—Home

Relax your breath and let your body breathe.

Inhale—Grace
Exhale—Home

Until you are asleep.

I have used this technique for many years. I use it now. Over the years I have changed the words. You may need to work with different words until you find what works best for you now. Know that you may change the words as you change.

# 13

# Practice Until You Want to Practice

Now that you are familiar with the what and whys of relaxation practice, let's turn to the how long, where, and how. You'll find the routine is much less tedious than you may expect. In fact, you're likely to discover that you can regularly practice your favorite exercise or several of them and still have a life!

### How long should you practice?
Only five minutes in the morning and five minutes at night! No music teacher would say that two five-minute segments a day could get you to Carnegie Hall. Nor would a baseball coach tell you this practice schedule could get you into the major leagues. Yet the fact remains that it will calm you down and it will change your life.

When I started reading books on relaxation, I was horrified to discover that I had to practice an hour a day or I would get nothing out of it. So I put the books down without even trying to build practice sessions into my life. Only later did I find out how wrong those books were—at least for the beginner I was then.

Eventually, when I did start practicing, I aimed for five minutes morning and night, but I didn't always make it. Then slowly it started to become a habit, and now I practice most mornings and most evenings. Occasionally, I'll lose track of time and my practice will go longer than usual or be very brief. What I learned is it's not so much the amount of time I devote to it as my pattern of consistently doing it.

Regularity is what breeds rewards—a formula I discovered while playing tennis. I'm not very good at the game, but because I like it, I don't let my lack of proficiency stop me from heading for the courts. Every time I play, I reap great gains—sunshine, fresh air, and physical exercise. No way must I be in the center court at Wimbledon to receive these fringe benefits; I need only make it a habit to lob the ball over the net a few times in a row. So it is with relaxation: after holding my point of focus for a few seconds and then starting over, I begin to feel good and my sessions have lengthened considerably and seemingly painlessly over the years.

As you get into the five-minute morning and evening relaxation routine, you might like the changes you feel and eventually decide to extend your practice sessions. If so, all the better. For now, however, plan on five minutes at a stretch—preferably first thing in the morning, before your mind is filled with thoughts, and just before you go to bed at night. Calming yourself at the start of the day will help smooth the edges of the chaos to come; at the close of the day, it will prepare you for a peaceful sleep.

### Where should you practice?

Wherever you're most comfortable! The living room or the den will do just fine or you might prefer to be outdoors under a tree, weather permitting. It often helps to have a spot set aside exclusively for your practice sessions. If you just happen to have an empty room in your house (joke), an entire room is ideal. The corner of a room will also work, as would any small space that is used for nothing else.

After a while you may want to begin decorating your spot. A special chair or cushion to sit on, or maybe a mat or pad, would make a good addition. Know that if you use the same couch, recliner, or rocking chair for relaxation that you sit in to watch Monday night football or to do needlepoint, you will still reap benefits from the practice. The key is comfort.

Nearby, you may want a small table to hold a candle, or a picture of a quiet, serene place in nature like Monument Valley is for me. Try flowers to look at, or the object you plan to hold. If you have not yet decided on an object to use as your point of focus, consider working with a rock or stick retrieved on a hike, or a seashell from a trip to the beach. Let the object help you recreate the place where you found it which can then become the image for your visualization.

### *How should you practice?*

First, your old friends: take those three slow breaths. As you begin to feel tranquil, move on to one of the longer exercises such as counting backward; or imagining yourself at the seashore; or focusing on a touch, scent, taste, sound, sight; or repeating your favorite poem. Another possibility would be to concentrate on your inhale and exhale, listening to the So-Hum sound of your breath.

Try not to let noises distract you. If you're doing your breathing exercises in your living room and hear a motorcycle pass by, you may think: "I wonder what kind of bike that is. Who's driving? Where is the person going? Oh, it's the guy next door. He's going to the diner for breakfast…They have great pancakes at the diner…I'd really like some pancakes right now…" Next thing you know, your mind will have you enjoying breakfast while your body is still in the living room.

Rather than let the sound of the motorcycle instigate an entire adventure, allow it to pass by your house (and your mind), and return to breathing. In other words, as soon as you realize you have been distracted, come back to what you were doing.

Internal distractions are also possible, especially nagging questions. If you begin to wonder, for example, "Should I have lunch with Bill tomorrow?" answer with a yes or no, then get back to your practice. Do not allow your mind to negotiate the question or to weigh both sides pro and con. Your mind will try, but don't go there. Resisting the mind chatter by refocusing is a big part of the exercise. You decide what you want to think about. After you have practiced this technique for a while, once the question is answered it will leave you alone.

### What if you want to practice at other times also?

By all means, do it. The idea is to start with the consistency of a small block of time in the morning and at night, and then see how you like it. When you get good results, you may want to add a session at noon, or at sunset, or on a purely spontaneous basis. In other words, encourage yourself to practice until you want to practice...then keep on practicing.

I used to practice breath exercises while sitting at my desk in the middle of a television production company in Hollywood. Two of the people I worked for made me crazy, and the breathing techniques returned me to sanity. You can do this, too. Here's how: While sitting at your desk, take thirty seconds to concentrate on the breath in your nostrils, nothing else, just your breath. It will give you a break from the rut you're in and also clear your mind.

One day just before a meeting with a difficult producer, I said to my boss, "Excuse me, I have to go to the bathroom." (Everyone is allowed two minutes in the bathroom, I figured.) I closed the stall door, sat on the toilet, and visualized myself at the seashore. There I saw the waves, felt the sun, and heard the gulls. I came back feeling quite refreshed!

If you excuse yourself to go to the "seashore" and then return to your office, the environment, the people, personalities, and politics will be just as crazy as they were when you left. You, however, will have changed. You will see the situation differently because your perception and your reaction to them will have changed. You'll be a little more serene and a lot less caught up in other people's emotions.

As you bring the practice of relaxation into your everyday life, consider the wondrous opportunities offered not only by the bathroom but also by your car. Try using your car as an auxiliary relaxation spot. To begin with, you could mentally convert your ignition button into your key to success. Just before you start your car—every time you start your car—stop and take three slow breaths. After you have stopped your car and turned off the ignition, take three slow breaths. Some people stick a red dot or gold star on their ignition button as a reminder to breathe.

These short pauses will change your attitude about driving. Soon both the anticipation of a nerve-wracking commute and the aftermath of a frustrating one will no longer jangle your nerves. You'll cruise along happy to take in the scenery and you'll return home with a smile. (This, of course, is a fantasy, but three slow breaths will help any commute.) As for on-the-road practice, when possible, substitute a new route for your usual one and you'll suddenly refocus on new sights in the visible world.

Opportunities for spontaneous relaxation practice are endless. For instance, you could write the word "breathe" on the backs of several of your business cards or on little slips of paper. Tuck one of these "breathe cards" in your wallet or purse, another in your coat pocket, and a few more in the pockets of your shirt and pants. Then anytime you reach into your wallet or a pocket and come across a card, do what it says: Take three slow breaths.

Use these techniques to relieve stress wherever and whenever it comes up. Stress, like vapors inside a teakettle, must be released from time to time; so, as pressure mounts, let it out through relaxation. Teakettles, on the other hand, have no such option. With the buildup of too much steam, they squawk and whistle their heads off.

Practicing any of these relaxation techniques for even two minutes will lift the lid of your kettle before your mouth shoots off. So go ahead and take a two-minute breather at your desk or in the bathroom or in your car; then go back to everyday life. Your boss or your teenager or whomever you are contending with will be as unreasonable as before. You, however, will be more calmed down, centered, and sane.

These techniques will work at the bus stop and on the loading dock. They'll work at midnight when you discover your exit is closed due to construction and on the Boeing 747 when the landing gear makes that awful noise on its descent. This is how we can de-stress during stressful times.

### PART THREE

# Going Deeper

# 14

# What Else Is Cooking?

A few years ago I stopped eating meat, not because some guru told me to, or to save the hogs and steers of the world, or even to help redistribute the planet's food supply. These are all admirable motives, but the reason I stopped eating meat was simply because I felt physically better without it. I hoped to enjoy a better quality of life. That's also why I practice relaxation: to have a better day, every day.

Soon after I changed my diet, a friend told me he didn't eat red meat, so I asked him if he was a vegetarian. "Heck, no!" he replied. "I don't eat my steaks red. I always have them well done." That was the day I realized how important it was to understand what people mean by the terms they use. My friend steered clear of red meat and I did, too…but we were on different paths. In the end, however, both our paths led straight to the kitchen.

So it is with relaxation. If two people tell you they use biofeedback, for example, ask what they actually do and why. One person may say she's using it to help herself alter her brain wave patterns or heart rate for purposes of stress management. The other may call it his tranquility process. The stress management you will understand from having practiced the relaxation techniques in Part One of this book. If you've trekked further down the road into the point-of-focus exercises in Part Two, you'll know about occupying the mind in order to achieve tranquility. "Yes, I know about that," you might reply to each of these people. "I call it relaxation." Before you know it, you'll all be in the "calm down kitchen" together discussing your favorite recipes for relaxation.

The point is that you're going to find differing terms and opinions about the pathways to relaxation. But there's no need to get proprietary about such matters. Just as you are likely to hear, "My God is the only God" in discussions about religion, so are you apt to hear in conversations about relaxation, "If you're not doing it my way, you're not really doing it." Your job is to stay open-minded and understanding. Who knows? Maybe you'll learn some helpful, new techniques.

The cause for this counsel is that something else is cooking: we are about to embark on an adventure even further down the road of relaxation. There are many names for this deeper practice. Dean Ornish M.D., in his best-selling book Eat More, Weigh Less, calls it "meditation" and offers seven reasons for giving it a try:

» First, meditation can enhance your powers of concentration.
» Second, it can increase your awareness of what's going on around you.
» Third, it can increase your awareness of what's going on inside you.
» Fourth, it can quiet your mind, allowing you to experience "inner sources of peace, joy, and nourishment."
» Fifth, it can give you a clearer picture of yourself.
» Sixth, it can draw you into the present moment, helping you experience new ways of being.
» Last, and perhaps most important, "meditation can give you the direct experience of transcendence, perhaps the most powerful way to deal with isolation."

Are these areas of life you would like to improve upon? If so, even if meditation is the last thing you're interested in exploring, take a slow breath and read on...The stew pot is boiling over with possibilities!

## 15

# The "M"-Word

W e have been talking about calming down and relaxing, and now the M word—meditation. Is there a difference? Absolutely, and that's what you're about to discover, but first, let's pick up where we left off at the end of Part II.

Once you've gotten all tranquil and serene from your point of focus exercises, should you keep practicing? Yes, because if you stop, you'll begin to lose the benefits, and in a very short time you'll start feeling steam building up again in your kettle. Keep practicing, however, and your mind will become even quieter. Another big bonus is that the number of unproductive or negative thoughts will decrease while positive to neutral thoughts will increase.

But, beware or be aware, the M word is used for many of the techniques you have already learned and practiced:

point of focus or the repetition of a word or phrases in English or foreign languages, for example, and dozens of other techniques. All of these point of focus exercises (notice I used the word exercises) are just that, concentration exercises to build your muscle of concentration. The byproduct is they are calming for our minds and bring a sense of peace and tranquility.

After you've practiced for a while longer, you'll be able to sit quietly, concentrating on a point of focus, a word or phrase, a sound or a smell, with no expectation of what might happen and no criticism of what does happen. You will cross the threshold into meditation and invite wondrous things to happen.

You will see that when you go past or through point-of-focus exercises you'll reach a place as if you are merging with what you have been concentrating on.

Meditation, in one way, is like sleep: we cannot will ourselves to sleep. We set up the proper circumstances for it—meditation or sleep—to happen, and it either does or it doesn't.

Hence, in choosing your point-of-focus object, consider something more significant to you than a new dress or a bright red Corvette. The more sacred or significant the object is to you, the more it will touch your heart.

As world-renowned mythologist Joseph Campbell said when asked if he believed in a "Higher Power," "I don't need to believe, I have experience." Campbell called it "Higher Power." Others call it the "Great Mystery" or "Amazing Grace" and with meditation that feeling of connectedness will deepen.

Although meditation is now used as a term for a stress reducer, the ancient teachers developed it for a different purpose—namely, as Dr. Ornish said, to give us a direct experience of transcendence (Beyond Human Experience), making it immanent (Existing Within) or merging with the Great Mystery.

But don't take my word for all this. Check it out yourself; practical experience is the best teacher.

Meditation is what happens in the gaps between thoughts. We can also find it in the gaps between breaths, those short transitions between exhale and inhale in which nothing happens—no moving, no breathing, no thinking—if only for half a second.

Now we are going to lengthen those gaps between thoughts, extending the time span in which we are comfortable with nothing happening to occupy our minds. And strange as it may sound, we will accomplish this by crossing the threshold from doing to feeling.

Here's a good way to think of it. If we go back to the example of walking in the woods, you'll recall that part of paying attention was the feeling you had of being connected to nature. The Vibration of Nature that sometimes feels like a comfortable, familiar, sympathetic vibration inside of us. If we use that vibration as our point of focus, concentrate on that feeling, maybe–or sometimes–we can have that same experience as Campbell.

For me, holding onto this feeling of connectedness is much easier in the woods than at home in the middle of the city. Yet no matter where I am, the feeling is accessible to me through meditation.

"Why would I want to do that?" you may ask. Because the pause is the doorway to our true essence, and as we step through it, at least two other things will begin to happen. The first is that sooner or later, in meditation, we will feel a sense of connectedness, the same inexplicable way we can feel connected to the Vibration of Nature in the forest, at the beach or in the desert. The second result is that we will discover something very meaningful about our own place in the world. Together, these two experiences add up to a revelation, or Self-Realization.

## EXERCISE XIV

# Going Deeper

### *How do we do this?*

By simply going to our center and feeling for our own vibration. To get there, I conjure up the vibration of nature or sounds or words which are meaningful, even sacred, to me. This is an exercise that begins with, but goes beyond, a point of focus. It helps if you also don't critique what comes up. Just observe it and see what comes up next.

First, read it through to learn what it's about. Then try it while reading the instructions. The third time, close your eyes and do the exercise while talking yourself through it.

This time try to sit up straight, but be relaxed. Take three slow breaths.

Place your right hand over your heart and your left hand over your right hand. Feel the gentle rise and fall of your chest as you inhale and exhale. Maybe you can feel your own heartbeat. If not, just for a second, touch your neck or wrist to feel your pulse, the beat of your own heart.

Did you know your heart began beating about forty-five days after you were conceived? Your heart synchronized itself with your mother's heartbeat and began beating, just as your mother's heart synchronized with her mother's and so on all the way back to the first mother's heart. Think about this as a sympathetic vibration, much like your own inner vibration and the Vibration of Nature.

Take a few more breaths and then close your eyes.

Become aware of the spot where your breath enters and leaves your nostrils. Continue to concentrate on this spot as you take a few more gentle breaths.

Now begin to follow your breath with your attention. Inhale and, as you do, feel the air in your nose, all the while seeing it in your mind's eye.

Feel the energy of your breath as it goes up from your nostrils to touch the inside top of your head, and then down a vertical passageway to a spot behind your hands. Feel the gentle rise of your chest under your hands.

Exhale, and as you do, feel the breath move up the passageway to the top of your head then out through your nostrils. Feel the lowering of your chest under your hands.

Inhale...in and down to your heart under your hands.

Exhale...up from your heart and out your nostrils.

Take a few more gentle breaths.

At the end of each inhale, stay for a second or two in the area of your heart.

Begin to 'Feel' your center of compassion and kindness.

Finally, ride your breath down to the area of your heart. Take your attention, your awareness, to your heart and stay there. Rather than being in your head looking down, ride your breath down until you are behind your palms—Be There.

Relax your arms and rest your hands comfortably.

With each exhale relax into this quiet place and feel for the Vibration of Nature inside you and your own vibration. It's as if your intuition is telling you these are the same vibrations, just as your brand-new heart had a sympathetic vibration with your mother's. Through our intuition, not our thinking, we develop faith that this is true.

For me, this is the feeling, the experience of Campbell's "Higher Power," the "Great Mystery," or "Amazing Grace." National publications called it the God Gene in each of us. Whatever you would like to call it, this vibration or experience can fill the void created by our feeling of aloneness. It can give us a sense of belonging to/with something larger than our small selves. There will be more on this in the next chapter.

Stay for a while with the feeling of being a part of **"All That Is."**

When you are ready slowly deepen your breathing, then open your eyes. Take your time. As you practice the experience will deepen.

Enjoy.

# 16

# The Stuff of the Universe

The first promise of meditation is it brings a feeling of connectedness with the world. It dispels the sense of aloneness.

Have you ever been through a time of feeling all alone? Do these sentiments sound familiar to you?

"My separateness, my aloneness, has always been with me and is here now, a recurring theme that has continuously run through my life. My closeness with Mama didn't change it...Aloneness is an inner state...Even now, with my three beautiful daughters, my two sweet sons, and my wonderful, sexy husband, deep down inside I am still profoundly alone."

That is the voice of Diana Ross, as chronicled in her memoir, Secrets of a Sparrow. If Diana Ross—one of the wealthiest, most talented, and most beautiful women in America—feels profoundly alone, what chance do you and I have of feeling otherwise?

To be sure, there are times when I feel all alone. Oh, I have a wonderful girlfriend and close friends; but I sometimes feel a gnawing emptiness inside me, a sense of "not belonging" in the world. On a deep-down level, other people can't make me feel okay. Nor can my job or my bank account or a new car or the new shoes I bought last week. The shoes were great the day I bought them, and even the first few times I wore them, but soon afterward, being the proud owner of these very cool new shoes did not help me feel like a valued member of society. The new car made me feel good for several weeks, but sure enough, that thrill wore off, too.

So, what shall I do? Buy new shoes each week and a car every month? Trade in my girlfriend every two or three years? Even if I get a promotion at work, the feeling of fulfillment will last only a little while. Then I'll need another promotion, and another, until I'm the CEO. At that point I'll need to find a bigger company so I can become CEO of that one.

If I am always on the search for "more," "bigger," "better," and "different" that need I can't fill will soon have me chasing my own tail. How many jobs, cars, and women must I go through before realizing that my life is not working, that I've done everything the television commercials told me to do and I'm no more fulfilled than I was at the start?

When asked by an interviewer who he preferred having as patients, the wealthy or the indigent, Carl Jung replied, "the wealthy."

Expecting an altruistic answer, the journalist asked why?

Jung replied he "preferred counseling people with money because they already knew that money alone wouldn't make them happy."

"Half my work was done," he added.

It takes more than just money and all the things it can buy to make us happy. Don't get me wrong, I believe in the old adage of "I've been rich, and I've been poor, and rich is better." Money and all the things it can buy, especially free time, make our lives much easier to live on many levels. But, on a Spiritual or Soul level, money won't buy our way into heaven. Money won't calm all of our inner turmoil. There are too many unhappy rich people in the world for any of us to believe that money, and only money, will make us happy.

How can I make my life work? Simple—by meditating and connecting to an inner source. After all, if I can't get what I need from the outside, the only place left to look is inside.

With meditation, remember, we're beyond thinking. We're feeling the other stuff—the essence that dwells within us. This feeling is actually a knowing that oozes through every cell of our being. It may not be an overwhelming feeling, and it may come on just a little at a time, yet however it happens we don't think our way into it. When we are quiet and connected enough, our intuition tells us it is so. Through meditation, we know it.

That's what happened for me after slipping between my thoughts and dropping down to the center of my being. A few weeks into this practice I found a vibration of unity—primal unity. Not the primal aloneness I experience when I'm up in my head, but a unity with all things...and I do mean all things.

This vibration is hard to describe, so I'll portray it conceptually. Quantum physicists tell us that the space between the atoms of our bodies is composed of the same "stuff" that makes up the space between the planets in our solar system and the space between the solar systems in our galaxy. It's the same "stuff" that makes up the space in the entire universe! The sympathetic vibration that came to me in meditation assured me that I am composed of the same stuff as the universe. Just as I had felt connected to the Vibration of Nature while in the woods, I could now feel connected to all that is—a oneness with all things in the universe.

Define the meaning of stuff however you will. A mystical or spiritual person might say there is an all-pervading spirit that is in and of the universe and is therefore a part of us. Wallace D. Wattles, a late-nineteenth-century scholar of Mind Science, wrote, "There is a thinking 'stuff' from which all things are made, and which, in its original state, permeates, penetrates, and fills the inter-spaces of the universe." A religious person would say that it is God, that they have a piece of God inside them, that their soul is a piece of God, that they are a child of God, and that they are connected to all living beings in the universe because of their connection to God.

All the energy in the universe is the same. Name it whatever you like; call it stuff, Spirit of the Universe, Vibration of Nature, Higher Power, Amazing Grace, the Great Mystery, God, or anything you wish. The point is that you don't need a religion to discover the existence of this energy. What it takes is meditation—dropping down inside and being there with no expectation of what might arise and no criticism of what does arise. Just feel the vibration and take it as it comes.

## 17

## Your Place in It All

The last chapter may have seemed a little thick or dense to you. That's because it is. But don't let that deter you forever. If these notions of energy and vibration are too mumbo jumbo for you, forget this section for now and come back to it later or in six months or a year. The words may have a different ring to them after you've practiced relaxation techniques for a while longer. And, once in a while, remind yourself how far you have come in a short time.

Here's a brief recap: remember that in addition to feeling a connectedness to the world, the other phenomenon that sooner or later will arise in meditation is an answer to the age-old question, "What is my place in the world?"

At some point, every person wonders, "What am I supposed to be doing with my life?" Native Americans go on vision quests to find answers to this dilemma; monks spend days in prayer; and some people pay a lot of money for years of therapy. Meditation, too, gives us an intuitive idea of what's best for us. We need only listen for an answer to this question. We would do well to phrase it in more immediate terms such as "What should I do today?"

Intuition is like a muscle—the more we exercise it, the stronger and more reliable it becomes. We have good intuition if we will just be quiet, listen, and not think. Remember the First Date story: you knew! When you are ready, go back and try again and see what bubbles up.

In addition, meditation can help us remember what we are not. For example, you are not your mind. You are also not your job; you do your job, but you are not your job. Neither are you anything else outside of you, such as shoes, cars, or your house. Although you may love these aspects of your life, and even wear them like a badge of honor, they are not us. Meditation gives us a new perspective on our lives.

Here's another benefit of meditation: by staying with the feeling that we are part of the universe, we will come to a feeling of "having enough." No longer will we think we need, like I did, more jobs, cars and shoes. Instead, we will have switched from a mindset of competition for the little there is in the world to one of gratitude, for what I have, be it a little or a lot and for all that is, knowing that in fact there is more than enough. Gratitude is the key to happiness. When I'm happy, that doesn't make me feel grateful, but when I feel grateful it always makes me feel happy. Here is a story about being grateful I found in a magazine years ago.

The story is about a Zen master named Sono who taught one very simple method of enlightenment. She advised everyone who came to her to adopt an affirmation to be said many times a day, under all conditions. The affirmation was

*"Thank you for everything. I have no complaint whatsoever."*

Many people from all arenas of life came to Sono for healing. Some were in physical pain; others were emotionally distraught; others had financial troubles; some were seeking soul liberation. No matter what their distress or what question they asked her, her response was the same:

*"Thank you for everything. I have no complaint whatsoever."*

Some people went away disappointed; others grew angry; others tried to argue with her. Yet some people took her suggestion to heart and began to practice it. Tradition tells that everyone who practiced Sono's mantra found peace and healing.

*"Thank you for everything. I have no complaint whatsoever."*

All of this is waiting for you on the inside…whenever you are ready give deeper meditation a try.

# 18

# Tune into Your Life

Have you ever missed dinner? I don't mean because you were too busy to eat or too late getting home; I mean while you were sitting right there at the dinner table with your family or friends.

I have. I am capable of tasting only the first bite of dinner, because after that my mind is off and running. "You eat dinner," it says. "I've got some thinking to do." (Remember breathing and counting at the same time?) Then, before I know it, my plate is empty, dinner is over…and having paid no attention to it, I missed the entire feast!

To prevent such distractedness, cultures around the world begin their meals with a prayer of thankfulness for the food set before them. There is a Zen saying, "How you do anything is how you do everything." When we rush through meals, we are likely to rush through life…When we can practice eating with awareness, then we are more likely to begin living with greater awareness. In this context, meditation not only enhances the experience of eating; eating with awareness becomes a form of meditation.

Through eating with awareness, I was able to shed the feeling that *food was my best friend*. I began eating to live rather than living to eat and overeat to feel full of affection from my best friend. The outcome was, slowly and safely, I lost weight.

Paying attention one moment at a time happens in the gap between thoughts. That's where we notice what's going on. Otherwise, we're thinking and not paying attention. When I am thinking, I'm not in the present moment; I'm not living my life; I'm living in the past or in the future. When I am paying attention, what happened yesterday does not matter; what matters is the present moment, each present moment. Lack of attention can be remedied by— here it is again—what the Buddhists call mindfulness.

When we are in that state of mindfulness (paying attention), we find meaning—worthwhileness—in everything we do, because we do it completely, wholeheartedly. To achieve this mindful way of being, simply tune in to whatever it is you are doing and try as best you can to have a really good attitude about it. Just as being grateful will make us happy, a good attitude will make us grateful. Here is a story about how a good attitude gives meaning* to our task.

*For more on Meaning see *Man's Search for Meaning, Copyright, Viktor E. Frankl 1959.*

The great Italian psychiatrist Roberto Assagioli wrote a parable about interviewing three stonecutters building a cathedral in the 14th century. The effect of their sense of personal meaning of their experience of their work is the same as the effect meaning has for us today.

When he asks the first stonecutter what he is doing, the man replies with bitterness that he is cutting stone into blocks, 1'x1'x1/2'. With frustration, he describes a life in which he has done this over and over, and will continue to do so until he dies.

The second man is also cutting stones 1'x1'x1/2', but he replies in a somewhat different way. With warmth, he says he is earning a living for his beloved family. Through his work his children have clothes and food to grow strong, and he and his wife have a home, that is filled with love.

But it is the third man whose response gives pause. In a joyous voice, he tells us of the privilege of participating in the building of this great cathedral, so strong it will stand as a holy lighthouse for a thousand years.

All three of the expert stonecutters are doing the same repetitive task: cutting stones. Finding meaning in a familiar task often allows us to go beyond this and find in the most routine tasks a deep sense of joy and even gratitude.

By not paying attention, we can lose great chunks of our lives. The challenge is to live our life one moment at a time. Whether you believe you have only one life to live or a series of them, live this one as if it were our one and only life.

Eventually, your relaxation practice will lead naturally into meditation practice. So, begin paying attention in the morning while you're in your meditation spot, far from worldly distractions. Think of this morning practice as a rehearsal for the rest of the day.

In time, you'll be able to practice paying attention, or Mindfulness, while out in the world. For instance, when your spouse, boss, or a friend speaks to you, avoid the temptation to prepare your reply and then jump in with it when the other person stops only to take a breath. Instead, listen to that person completely, word for word, and then formulate your response. Think of this approach as paying attention, one word at a time.

Taoists, followers of sixth-century BCE Chinese philosophy, also speak of this phenomenon. They say there is an invisible, unspoken Way in which the world unfolds, and our job is to come into harmony with it. But if it's invisible and nobody talks about it, you may ask, how can we come into harmony with it?

Here, again, the answer is, by paying attention. When we tune into the world around us, we discover there is a pulse in things inanimate as well as animate. For example, while operating a machine such as a car or sewing machine, we may at first think we're the ones in control, but actually we're working in partnership with the machine. Although we may read the owner's manual, the machine itself is apt to be the best teacher.

When we pay close attention to the machine, it will tell us how it performs best and how it wants to be used. Sure, we can try to impose our will on it, but the results are likely to be disappointing. If we relax and feel our way while driving the car, for instance, we will soon come into harmony with it. If we try to make it work the way we want it to—if we try to push the river, so to speak—the outcome may be disastrous. The same is true of a sewing machine. The larger the machine, the more obvious this becomes. Imagine driving not a family passenger car but an 18-wheeler. I would truly want to be in harmony with something that heavy lest I lose "control." As in other areas of my life, if I tried to make a situation go my way, it either didn't at all or took much longer than my game plan called for. And that appears to be the lesson of life itself. If we remain sensitive to our surroundings, we soon fall into the natural rhythm of living.

When I'm not paying attention to what's going on around me, for example, I "bump into" life, in the form of a doorjamb or the rear end of the car in front of me. If I'm paying attention to my surroundings instead of trying to push the river, I have an easier time of it.

Thought and action go hand in hand to make us who we are. Why is this so? Because who we are today is a result of what we did in the past. Similarly, who we will become is a result of our current thoughts, since what we think ultimately determines what we will do. Hence, we think...we act...we become.

It follows that the great changes we would like to make in our lives result from the changes we bring to our thinking. And if our thinking is negative, the easiest way to effect desirable results is through positive actions.

This may sound roundabout, but watch how it works: Maybe I have negative thoughts about myself and would like to deepen my self-respect. Then if I behave (positive actions) in ways that will increase my respect for myself, I cultivate (positive thinking).

One positive action that can profoundly influence who we will become is the practice of relaxation techniques that will sooner or later lead us into meditation. All the benefits of calming down will flow through us, including a quiet mind, serenity, and inner peace. In this frame of mind, we will feel good inside and deeply connected to the world around us, leading eventually to positive actions and a new us.

## POINTS TO REMEMBER

» Don't confuse techniques with meditation. Counting backward and watching a candle flame are relaxation techniques; meditation happens in the pause between thoughts. Meditation happens as we go past techniques and out of thought.

» Meditation happens as we mindfully live our lives, paying attention to each moment.

» Life is The Meditation. Good days, bad days, it's our life—live every moment of it!

» Even if you're absolutely, totally nuts today, tomorrow we can revel in peace of mind.

Well, there you have it. A game plan, a blueprint, a call to action for a more peaceful and enjoyable life. As I promised at the beginning of our journey, my hope is that these baby steps we took together, simple and easy exercises, will help you move into a more comfortable way of living. You may want to reread the seemingly denser sections of this book. They will come to serve you well, just as three slow breaths will serve you well for the rest of your life. Thank you for making me a part of your life. It has truly been my pleasure to travel a short distance on the road with you.

Vaya con Dios…

# 19

# Fred's Everyday Stress Tips

STRESS. An unreasonable or overwhelming demand on the nervous system.

1. Live today only. Cling to no animosity regarding yesterday. Holding a resentment is like drinking poison and waiting for the other person to die. Take three slow breaths.

2. Take a slow breath and say a short affirmation, prayer or mantra. Take two slow breaths. Continue breathing.

3. Carry with you something small that reminds you of peaceful times—a lucky charm or a talisman. When agitated, pull your object out of your pocket or purse and hark back to a moment of tranquility.

4. Sit down, close your eyes, and visualize yourself in your favorite place in nature. Use all of your sense memories.

5. Step outside. Feel the sun on your face. Say Thank You for the day.

6. Laugh out loud and decide to be happy. As Abraham Lincoln said, "Most folks are as happy as they make up their minds to be." Laughing makes us breathe deeper.

### Worry not. Here's why—take your pick.

1. My grandmother said worry was like her rocking chair. It gave her something to do but it didn't get her anywhere.
2. There is a Tibetan proverb: "If a problem has a solution, there is no need to worry about it. If there is no answer for the problem, worry will do no good."
3. My grandfather said worry was a way of praying for what you *don't* want.

### Fred's Rules of Non-Engagement

1. Avoid arguments in general, but especially with people who are not in the room with you.
2. Do not engage.
3. If engaged, do not escalate.
4. Never, ever pass up a good opportunity to Shut the F**k Up.

## *Holiday Stress Tips*

Holiday Stress—Family and friends not doing what you want, how you want it done, when you feel it needs to be done.

Remember the reason for the season. Whether your season is Christmas, Hanukkah, Kwanzaa, or simply to add a little light to the longest night of the year, take one deep breath and remember why you are here.

Place a symbol of the season in plain sight, e.g. on your desk or the kitchen table.

Call a friend and wish them Happy Holidays.

Steer clear of holiday arguments by not giving other people directions. As Mark Twain said, "I don't need anyone to tell me what to do. I already don't do half the things I know I should do."

# Notes

*Chapter 14*

1. Dean Ornish, Eat More, Weigh Less (New York: Harper Collins, 1993), p. 78.

*Chapter 16*

1. Diana Ross, Secrets of a Sparrow: Memoirs (New York: Villard Books, 1993), p. 229.

2. Wallace D. Wattles, The Science of Getting Rich (Lakemont, GA: Copple House Books, 1975), p. 110.

## ABOUT THE AUTHOR

# Fred L. Miller

Fred L. Miller is a teacher and the author of the Top Ten Best Selling *How To Calm Down Even If You're Absolutely, Totally Nuts*, and the 20th Anniversary Edition—Revised & Updated. The twenty-five years he spent in television production in both blue-collar and white-collar jobs was a  life that drove him absolutely nuts until he learned to calm down. He has written for prime-time network television and produced and directed documentary and educational films. His stint at a large New York advertising agency is what almost drove him over the edge.

To save his own life he has spent thirty-five years acquiring esoteric knowledge and has devoted the last thirty to making that knowledge accessible in everyday terms. Calming down is what saved his sanity and facilitated a long, successful career in the entertainment industry.

He has lectured on breath awareness at the UCLA School of Medicine, has taught relaxation techniques to cancer patients and is certified by the California State Bar Association to teach attorneys meditation as stress management. Also, Blue Cross of California listed him as a preferred provider in complementary medicine.

Fred is also a student of Tai Chi, Chi Gong, Aikido, Alexander Technique and Feldenkrais. He has traveled and studied in India, Nepal, Tibet, Bhutan, Jerusalem, and the Rain Forest of Peru.

Fred earned a BA in Communications from San Francisco State University. He is an Executive Coach certified through the Professional School of Psychology by the state of California and a member of the Writers Guild of America, Directors Guild of America, and PEN.

*How To Calm Down*
*Even if You're Absolutely, Totally Nuts*

Have questions? Want to learn more?—
www.howtocalmdown.com

Printed in Great Britain
by Amazon

18997991R00086